6/2001

W9-AUD-751

Rabbits Have Bunnies

by Lynn M. Stone

Animals and Their Young

Content Adviser: Terrence E. Young Jr., M.Ed., M.L.S.
Jefferson Parish (La.) Public Schools

Reading Adviser: Dr. Linda D. Labbo,
Department of Reading Education, College of Education,
The University of Georgia

COMPASS POINT BOOKS

Minneapolis, Minnesota

Compass Point Books
3722 West 50th Street, #115
Minneapolis, MN 55410

For more information about Compass Point Books, e-mail your request to:
custserv@compasspointbooks.com

Photographs ©: Lynn M. Stone

Editors: E. Russell Primm and Emily J. Dolbear
Photo Researcher: Svetlana Zhurkina
Photo Selector: Linda S. Koutris
Design: Bradfordesign, Inc.

Library of Congress Cataloging-in-Publication Data

Stone, Lynn M.
      Rabbits have bunnies / by Lynn Stone.
          p. cm. — (Animals and their young)
      Includes bibliographical references and index.
      Summary: Describes the appearance and behavior of baby rabbits from birth to eight weeks.
      ISBN 0-7565-0005-2 (lib. bdg.)
          1. Rabbits—Infancy—Juvenile literature. [1. Rabbits. 2. Animals—Infancy.] I. Title. II. Series:
Stone, Lynn M. Animals and their young.
SF453.2 .S825 2000
636.9'322—dc21
                                                                                            00-008835

Table of Contents

What Are Bunnies?

Bunnies are baby rabbits. At two weeks old, they are bright eyed and furry. But they don't begin life that way! Newborn rabbits cannot see or hear. They have no hair at all.

Bunnies are born to does and bucks. A **doe** is a mother rabbit. A **buck** is a father rabbit. This book is about bunnies born on farms and bunnies born to pet rabbits.

A mother rabbit is called a doe.

How Do Bunnies Arrive?

Baby rabbits are usually born in the early spring or late fall. A doe has four to six bunnies. Together the babies make up the doe's **litter**.

The bunnies begin to grow inside the mother rabbit after she has mated with a buck. After about one month, they are born in a nest of fur and straw.

The mother rabbit keeps her babies cozy in her long, warm fur. Without her, the baby rabbits couldn't live.

Week-old bunnies rest in their nest.

How Do Bunnies Feed?

Newborn bunnies feel the need to suck. This is a natural **instinct**. When bunnies are born, the doe doesn't teach the bunnies how or where to find food. They know how and where to eat by instinct.

Newborn bunnies wriggle around to find their mother's milk. Drinking their mother's milk is called **nursing**.

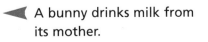 A bunny drinks milk from its mother.

What Do Bunnies Eat?

Newborn bunnies don't eat any solid food.
They live on their mother's milk.

Mother's milk is healthy for baby rabbits.
The milk has fat, proteins, vitamins, and other
things to help the rabbits grow.

◄ Bunnies grow by drinking their
mother's milk.

What Do Newborn Bunnies Do?

Tiny newborn bunnies can't see or hear. Their eyes are shut tight. They can't hop yet either. Bunnies stay near the mother even as they grow larger. The mother rabbit is a warm blanket and a warm meal!

◀ Newborn bunnies can't go very far.

What Does a Bunny Look Like?

A newborn rabbit is about the length of your smallest finger. There are many different sizes and kinds, or **breeds**, of rabbits. The largest breeds have the largest babies.

Newborn bunnies are pink. They have no hair. They don't even have a short, fluffy rabbit tail yet. But their ears and their back feet are already long!

Bunnies begin to look fuzzy when they are only two days old. In about seven to ten days, they have a coat of soft fur.

◀ This bunny looks a lot like a grown-up rabbit.

What Do Young Rabbits Do and Eat?

Young rabbits quickly become bigger and more active. By the time they are two weeks old, they look just like full-grown rabbits.

At two weeks, a bunny is as furry as its mother. It has bright eyes and long, fuzzy ears. It twitches its nose just like its parents do.

Now it has the energy to play and hop. It still needs its mother's milk, but it doesn't need her warmth as often.

Young rabbits can be very curious.

What Happens As a Rabbit Grows Older?

Bunnies nurse for eight weeks. At that age, they are old enough to eat rabbit food and drink water.

At the age of four to five weeks, bunnies can eat rabbit chow. This food looks like little brown pellets. But it is full of healthy, ground-up foods. At eight weeks, bunnies get almost all their food from these dry, crusty pellets.

◄ Bunnies eat pellets called rabbit chow.

When Is a Young Rabbit Grown Up?

Rabbit pellets help keep a young rabbit healthy. Sometimes, rabbits enjoy a slice of apple or pear, maple leaves, grassy hay, or a piece of carrot.

By the time it is four or five months old, a rabbit is grown up. It has a fur coat as thick as its mother's. Soon it will be ready to have bunnies of its own. With a good start in life, rabbits may live to be five or six years old.

◀ A healthy rabbit can live a long life.

Glossary

breeds—kinds of rabbits or other animals

buck—an adult male rabbit; a father rabbit

doe—an adult female rabbit; a mother rabbit

instinct—knowing what to do without being taught; a natural behavior

litter—a group of animals born to one mother at the same time

nursing—drinking milk produced by the mother

Did You Know?

- Baby rabbits are also called kits.

- Jackrabbits can run about 45 miles (72 kilometers) per hour.

- A jackrabbit can jump about 15 to 20 feet (4.6 to 6 meters) in a single leap.

Want to Know More?

At the Library

Barrett, Norman S. *Rabbits*. New York: Franklin Watts, 1990.

Burton, Jane. *Freckles the Rabbit*. New York: Random House, 1988.

Coldrey, Jennifer. *The World of Rabbits*. Milwaukee: Gareth Stevens, 1986.

On the Web

House Rabbit Society

http://www.rabbit.org/

For information about the nonprofit organization that rescues rabbits and educates people about rabbit care

How to Care for Your Rabbits

http://www.oink.demon.co.uk/pets/rabbits.htm

For tips on keeping rabbits as pets

Through the Mail

American Rabbit Breeders Association

P.O. Box 426

Bloomington, IL 61702

For information about raising rabbits

On the Road

County fairs are a great place to meet people who raise rabbits for pets. These fairs are usually held in midsummer or late summer.

Index

About the Author

Lynn M. Stone has written hundreds of children's books and many articles on natural history for various magazines. He has photographed wildlife and domestic animals on all seven continents for such magazines as *National Geographic, Time, Ranger Rick, Natural History, Field and Stream*, and *Audubon*.

Lynn Stone earned a bachelor's degree at Aurora University in Illinois and a master's degree at Northern Illinois University. He taught in the West Aurora schools for several years before becoming a writer-photographer full-time. He lives with his wife and daughter in Batavia, Illinois.